INSTRUCTIVE MOMENTS WITH THE SAVIOR

Learning to hear

KEN GIRE

ZondervanPublishingHouse
Grand Rapids, Michigan

A Division of HarperCollins*Publishers*

Instructive Moments with the Savior
Copyright © 1992 by Ken Gire

Requests for information should be addressed to:
Zondervan Publishing House
Grand Rapids, Michigan 49530

Library of Congress Cataloging in Publication Data

Gire, Ken.
    Instructive moments with the Savior : learning to hear / Ken
Gire.
        p.   cm.
    ISBN 0-310-54970-1 (alk. paper)
        1. Jesus Christ—Parables—Meditations. 2. Bible. N.T.
Gospels—Meditations. I Title.
    BT375.2.G57   1992
    242'.5—dc20   92-26637
                                                          CIP

Published in association with the literary agency of Sealy M. Yates and
Associates, Orange, California.

Printed in the United States of America

93 94 95 96 97 98 / DH / 12 11 10 9 8 7 6 5 4 3 2

This edition is printed on acid-free paper and meets the American
National Standards Institute Z39.48 standard.

edicated
affectionately to my children:

> To Gretchen, who encourages my faith.
> To Kelly, who deepens my feelings.
> To Rachel, who makes me laugh.
> To Stephen, who is a much better boy
> than I was.
> I am so proud of you all.

And I feel so privileged to be the one you call
"Dad."

CONTENTS

Introduction ix

An Instructive Moment About Hearing 1

An Instructive Moment About Love 11

An Instructive Moment About Life 23

An Instructive Moment About Humility 33

An Instructive Moment About Forgiveness 41

An Instructive Moment About Our Father 51

An Instructive Moment About Prayer 61

An Instructive Moment About Death 69

An Instructive Moment About
    God's Kingdom 79

An Instructive Moment About Mercy 87

An Instructive Moment About Watchfulness ... 97

An Instructive Moment About Faithfulness 103

An Instructive Moment About the Patience
    of God 113

An Instructive Moment About Our Lives 123

"He who has ears

to hear,

let him hear."

INTRODUCTION

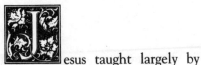esus taught largely by telling stories. The Bible calls them parables. With these homespun stories Jesus explained everything from the kingdom of heaven to how to be a good neighbor.

The stories are simple. They have more in common with the fables of Aesop than with the well-crafted sermons of today. With a once-upon-a-time magic to them, they weave a spell no sermon ever could.

They captivate us, yet they themselves refuse to be captured. Like flashes of lightning, they bolt into our imagination, and before we know it they are gone. What we are left with is a startling sense that something from heaven has come down and touched our lives—touched them in a thunderous way and unsettled them.

How the parable of the Good Samaritan must have unsettled the life of the legal expert who asked the question, "Who is my neighbor?"! Was he ever the same after that flash of the Savior's insight? Could he ever again just look at some helpless person on the street and walk away? Not without the thunder of the parable shaking the core of his being.

But not all parables come to us in such dramatic ways. Some slip into our lives as unassumingly as a seed slips from its pod and falls into the ground. Malcolm Muggeridge once said that every happening, great and small, is a parable whereby God speaks to us; and the art of life is to get the message.

That message comes to us in many ways, often in the most unexpected of ways, as when the Word became flesh. The Messiah born to an unwed mother? God's son cradled in a feeding trough? Can any good thing come out of Nazareth? Where did this man get this wisdom and these miraculous powers? Isn't this the carpenter's son?

Who ever heard of such things?

And yet there *were* those who heard of such things. They followed the Savior and loved him and gave their lives for him. They were the ones who learned that truth can be found in places you would never think to look. They were the ones who learned to hear.

Learning to hear. That's what this book is all about.

Maybe by learning to hear God's message in the parables, we can learn to hear his message in other areas of life as well: the wisdom that comes to us through suffering; the revelation that is spoken through the short-lived petals of a flower; the word to our conscience at the sight of another human being foraging for food in a garbage can.

When we begin to get those messages, we will begin to grasp the art of life.

As you cup your ears to the following chapters, you will notice that each instructive moment with the Savior begins with a passage of Scripture, is followed by few reflective comments, and ends with a prayer. You will notice too that the prayers are unfinished.

The prayers start a story only you can complete. It is a sacred story, one that has never been told before and one that will never be repeated again. It is the story of your life . . . a life that in time will itself become a parable whereby God speaks.

Ken Gire

AN
INSTRUCTIVE MOMENT
ABOUT HEARING

❧

SCRIPTURE

hile a large crowd was gathering and people were coming to Jesus from town after town, he told this parable:

."A farmer went out to sow his seed. As he was scattering the seed, some fell along the path; it was trampled on, and the birds of the air ate it up. Some fell on rock, and when it came up, the plants withered because they had no moisture. Other seed fell among thorns, which grew up with it and choked the plants. Still other seed fell on good soil. It came up and yielded a crop, a hundred times more than was sown."

When he said this, he called out, "He who has ears to hear, let him hear."

His disciples asked him what this parable meant. He said, "The knowledge of the secrets of the kingdom of God has been given to you, but to others I speak in parables, so that,

" 'though seeing, they may not see;
though hearing, they may not understand.'

"This is the meaning of the parable: The seed is the word of God. Those along the path are the ones who hear, and then the devil comes and takes away the word from their hearts, so that they may not believe and be saved. Those on the rock are the ones who receive the word with joy when they hear it, but they have no root. They believe for a while, but in the time of testing they fall away. The seed that fell among thorns stands for those who hear, but as they go on their way they are choked by life's worries, riches and pleasures, and they do not mature. But the seed on good soil stands for those with a noble and good heart, who hear the word, retain it, and by persevering produce a crop."

Luke 8:4–15

MEDITATION

esus has been traveling with his disciples along the northern tip of the Sea of Galilee, visiting the inland city of Korazin and the coastal cities of Bethsaida and Capernaum.

These cities have heard Jesus say some amazing things and seen him do things even more amazing. With a mere touch of his hand or a word from his mouth, the blind have received their sight, the lame have walked, the deaf have received their hearing. The people there have even seen Jesus raise the dead.

When he left these cities, they bobbed in a wake of controversy: "Is this miracle worker the Son of David or is he the Son of the Devil?"

Jesus is outside Capernaum now, where a crowd gathers on the seashore. They flock around him, eager and hopeful as gulls hovering over an incoming fishing boat. So great is the crush of the crowd that he finally has to step into a beached rowboat and push out from shore.

Lining the shore in front of him are his twelve disciples. The sloping, crescent shoreline forms an open amphitheater for the rest of the crowd. Capernaum lies to his right. To his left the Galilean sun lies in a nest of hills like some huge golden egg. Behind him, anchored boats with naked masts rock lazily in the lapping water. The breeze is cool and carries with it the memory of this morning's catch. A kingfisher sails kite-like over the water, swoops down to spear its dinner, then wings away from the crowd to a secluded stretch of beach.

Jesus sits down in the bow of the boat, the blue sea

॰

surrounding him slowly deepening in color, as if sombered by the words that are to come.

Jesus calls to hush the crowd: "He who has ears to hear, let him hear."

The disciples anticipate another message like the Sermon on the Mount. A well-crafted sermon with a rustic illustration or two for the common folk. Some insightful comments on a few Old Testament passages for the scholars. And a strong altar call at the end for everyone.

But when Jesus finishes speaking, the disciples tacitly cut their eyes at each other for an explanation. One by one they relay a shrug of shoulders.

After the crowd disperses, the puzzled disciples ask what the parable means. Jesus answers: "The knowledge of the secrets of the kingdom of God has been given to you, but to others I speak in parables so that, 'though seeing, they may not see; though hearing, they may not understand.'"

A parable is a kernel of spiritual truth surrounded by the husk of an earthly story. In the parables about God's kingdom, the mysteries of the kingdom are hidden in such a way so that sincere seekers will find the kernel of truth, while those who aren't will find only husk.

But why obscure the message? Why not make it as clear as possible so the greatest number of people can come into the kingdom?

Because Jesus has already given these people every

opportunity to hear the truth about the kingdom of God, and they have rejected it. When he recently healed a man on the Sabbath, the Pharisees plotted to kill him. When he cast a demon out of a possessed man, the religious leaders denounced him: "It is only by Beelzebub, the prince of demons, that this fellow drives out demons."

In a scathing indictment of their unbelief, Jesus proclaimed: "Woe to you, Korazin! Woe to you, Bethsaida! . . . And you, Capernaum . . . If the miracles that were performed in you had been performed in Sodom, it would have remained to this day. But I tell you that it will be more bearable for Sodom on the day of judgment than for you."

In a later incident the Pharisees tried to persuade Jesus to perform another miracle to convince their unbelieving eyes. That is when Jesus pronounced a final judgment on them, sealing not only their fate . . . but his.

"A wicked and adulterous generation asks for a miraculous sign! But none will be given it except the sign of the prophet Jonah. For as Jonah was three days and three nights in the belly of a huge fish, so the Son of Man will be three days and three nights in the heart of the earth."

When the king is rejected, the offer of the kingdom is withdrawn. And when Jesus goes to the cross, he will take the promise of the kingdom with him. Until he one day returns with that kingdom, he has restricted his reign on earth to the small field of the human heart.

❧

But as the parable indicates, the human heart is no easy field to cultivate. It is hard and rocky and full of weeds.

In the parable Jesus described the spiritual fields that make up the landscape of northern Galilee. In doing so, he explained to his disciples how he could spread the word of his kingdom throughout the land and there be such a varied response to his message.

Throughout the hills and valleys of the northern coast, there were hearts impervious to truth—the hearts of the scribes and Pharisees, for example, trodden by tradition and packed hard by the proud feet of their own righteousness.

There were hearts that embraced the truth, and sudden sprigs of spiritual life sprang up around the countryside like wildflowers after a rain. But with only a shallow commitment to the truth, their roots never grew very deep. And under the heat of testing, their faith withered. The leather-faced sailor, for example, who believed but whose faith buckled under the ridicule of his shipmates.

Then there were hearts where the roots ran deep. They sent up sturdy stalks that survived the sun. But a few seeds of worldliness were overlooked, their creeping vines tolerated, and before long the life of that sturdy stalk became stunted. The businessman from Korazin, for instance, who not only embraced the truth but followed Jesus all around the hill country, asking questions, learning, helping out whenever he could. But he finally decided it was time to get back to business. After all, his

☙

customers were depending on him, his competitors were catching up with him, and his creditors were coming after him. Besides, there was the mortgage on his vacation villa, the new boat he wanted to buy, and the comfortable life on the beach that beckoned him. Slowly, imperceptibly, the vines won out.

Then there were those patches of ground that every farmer lives for—a few hearts that were fertile and receptive to the truth, cleared of any obstacles to their commitment, weeded of any competing loves. In these hearts God's word germinated, quietly sent out its roots, and steadily grew. First the blade, then the stalk, then the head, then the full kernel in the head.

In each case in the parable, the productivity of the seed is dependent upon the receptivity of the soil.

Herein lies a mystery.

Why would God confine the boundless power of heaven to a few seeds of haphazardly scattered truth, burying the hopes for an eternal harvest in such uncertain soil as that of the human heart?

PRAYER

ear Lord of the Harvest, why is it that so little of the seed that is sown in my heart ever reaches maturity, let alone, fruition?

Why is it that your Word has such a hard time implanting itself in my life? Why do I wilt when my faith comes under heat? Why is it that week after week I'm hacking away at the same old weeds?

Come into my garden, Lord. Take your plow and furrow the hardness out of my life. Dig up the obstacles that keep the roots of my faith from growing deeper. Pull out the worldly preoccupations that tendril their thorns around my heart and squeeze out my spiritual life.

Cultivate my heart, Lord, so I may catch every word that falls from heaven. Every syllable of encouragement; every sentence of rebuke. Every paragraph of instruction; every page of warning. Help me to catch these words as the soft, fertile soil catches seeds.

Help me to watch over that heart with all diligence, realizing that the harvest of my heart not only helps to feed a generation now but to seed the harvests for generations to come. . . .

An
INSTRUCTIVE MOMENT
ABOUT LOVE

ي

n one occasion an expert in the law stood up to test Jesus. "Teacher," he asked, "what must I do to inherit eternal life?"

"What is written in the Law?" he replied. "How do you read it?"

He answered: " 'Love the Lord your God with all your heart and with all your soul and with all your strength and with all your mind'; and, 'Love your neighbor as yourself.' "

"You have answered correctly," Jesus replied. "Do this and you will live."

But he wanted to justify himself, so he asked Jesus, "And who is my neighbor?"

In reply Jesus said:

"A man was going down from Jerusalem to Jericho, when he fell into the hands of robbers. They stripped him of his clothes, beat him and went away, leaving him half dead. A priest happened to be going down the same road, and when he saw the man, he passed by on the other side. So too, a Levite, when he came to the place and saw him, passed by on the other side. But a Samaritan, as he traveled, came where the man was; and when he saw him, he took pity on him. He went to him and bandaged his wounds, pouring on oil and wine. Then he put the man on his own donkey, took him to an inn and took care of him. The next day he took out two silver coins and gave them to the innkeeper. 'Look after him,' he said, 'and when I return, I will reimburse you for any extra expense you may have.'

"Which of these three do you think was a neighbor to the man who fell into the hands of robbers?"

The expert in the law replied, "The one who had mercy on him."

Jesus told him, "Go and do likewise."

Luke 10:25–37

ॐ

MEDITATION

ho is my neighbor?

The question is asked by a lawyer trying more to settle an uneasy conscience than to settle a debate. He finds the answer to his question in the most unexpected of places—on a dusty road leading out of Jerusalem.

The road from Jerusalem to Jericho slopes steadily downward through a wilderness of rocks and ravines and crumbly outcroppings of limestone. The only color comes from the paint of the rising sun as it brushes a streak of pink across the chalky hills. The road snakes through those hills for seventeen miles, writhing perilously close to steep ravines and winding around bare shoulders of rock.

In the twists and turns of that road hide hardened criminals, lying in wait the way a tarantula waits for an unsuspecting beetle to fall into its trap. For that reason the road has earned the reputation as "The Way of Blood."

Down that road comes a tired priest. The robbers recognize him to be a religious man from the clothes he wears, and so they allow him safe passage. Some things are sacred, even to criminals. Besides, they reason, priests never carry anything of value anyway.

The priest walks with his back toward the eight days of service he has just given in the temple. From morning till evening he has served there, instructing the people in the straight-and-narrow ways of the Law. For the times they have strayed, he has made intercession. Burning incense. Saying prayers. Offering sacrifices. The days

&

have been long and tiresome with tedious attention to detail given to everything from trying legal cases to trimming the wicks of the temple's oil lamps.

But now he is off duty on his way home to Jericho, that lush, worldly suburb of the holy city.

The priest passes the time by meditating on a psalm, but the graceful rhythms of Hebrew poetry are jarred to a stop by the guttural moans coming from the roadside.

There lies a clump of naked flesh. The priest squints. It looks like a fellow Jew, but it's hard to tell. The man has been beaten raw, and a seepage of blood darkens the dirt beneath him.

The Law says that if you see your brother's donkey or ox fall down by the way, you should not hide yourself from it but should help it up. How much more, then, should you help if your brother himself has fallen?

But that's not the portion of the Law that comes to the priest's mind. He thinks of the passage which states that anybody who touches a dead person shall be rendered unclean for seven days.

The priest reasons to himself: The poor man's barely alive. If I stop and help him, he could die in my arms. Then he thinks of the elaborate ritual he would have to go through to purify himself, and frankly, he has had enough of rituals for one week. Besides, if the priest is rendered unclean, that would interfere with his religious duties at the local synagogue in Jericho, and he is slated to teach Torah classes all the next week.

ॐ

So instead of risking the defilement that would keep him from fulfilling his religious responsibilities, the priest turns and walks away. After all, teaching is his gift, and it wouldn't be a wise use of his talent to have to bury it for a week.

A Levite is the next to come down the road. As a subordinate to the priest, he assists in the temple worship. But he too is off work and anxious to get home.

His steps are brisk. He needs to be in Jericho by noon, in time for the city council meeting where he has been asked to give the opening invocation. It is an honor and an important step in his career. It will give him greater visibility and a greater circle of influence.

The opportunity should open a lot of doors for him. It's a good chance to rub shoulders with the council members and the top merchants. Good givers, those merchants. And they know how to treat their holy men. Once you get a little recognition, that is. And once you get in with the right people.

Yes, this is the opportunity he has been waiting for— to bring religion to the marketplace, to make a difference in the lives of the community's key leaders, and maybe to make a denarius or two on the side.

The Levite's mind dances with the possibilities. He thinks of speaking engagements that will come his way, of sitting at banquets in the seat of honor, of being invited to the best social functions, of being given luxurious imported goods at cost or, better still, being given them

❧

free as a token of someone's appreciation for his insightful teaching.

His steps grow brisk on the downward road to Jericho.

But his stride is broken as the bend in the road reveals the man who has been beaten by robbers. He looks at the man and then at the angle of the sun. He has to make Jericho by noon. He has a commitment to keep. Surely somebody will come along in a minute or two, he reasons as he picks up his pace and walks to the other side of the road.

Then comes a Samaritan riding his donkey down the dusty stretch of road. He has been in Jerusalem on business and is on his way to Jericho to complete some business there before returning home.

But the business climate in Judea is not favorable toward Samaritans. The Jews despise them. They don't receive them into their homes, believing that if they did they would be storing up curses upon their children. And they would no more eat at a Samaritan's table than they would at a swine's trough. The hatred is so intense that Jews publicly curse them in the synagogue, asking God to exclude them from eternal life.

The Samaritan tries to shake off the rude way he has been treated, having seen his own people treat Jews just as badly.

As he rounds a bend in the road, he sees the wounded man lying there. The Samaritan's heart compels him to stop. It is so full of compassion that it has no room for questions. The man is a Jew, but it makes no difference

જ

what race he is, or what religion, or what region of the country he is from. He's a human being in need, and as far as the Samaritan's concerned, that's all that matters.

From his heavily packed donkey he takes a wineskin and an earthen jar of oil. He rushes to the man's side and pours wine on his wounds to disinfect them and oil to soothe them. He tears strips from his garment to sop up the blood and to staunch the life that is ebbing away. Gingerly, he shoulders the man onto his donkey, steadying him as he walks by his side.

In a couple of miles they arrive at an inn. The Samaritan could just drop the man off, slip the innkeeper a night's rent, and leave. But he doesn't do that. He stays the night, watching over the wounded man during those first, critical twenty-four hours. Sponging him down. Changing his bandages. Giving him a few sips of water every time he regains consciousness.

The next day the Samaritan must be on his way, but the wounded man is in too critical a condition to travel. He empties his leather pouch. Into the innkeeper's palm clink two silver coins, an equivalent of two days' wages. The Samaritan not only goes out on a financial limb for the man, but he goes into debt, obligating himself for any expenses the innkeeper may incur in nursing this total stranger back to health.

As far as we know, the Samaritan did nothing for the stranger's soul. He uttered no prayer, quoted no verse, left no tract. All he did was to give the man the physical help he needed. And that seemed to be enough. At least it was enough in the eyes of the one who told the story.

~

In demonstrating what it meant to be a good neighbor, the Samaritan defined the meaning of love. Love doesn't look away. And it doesn't walk away. It involves itself. It inconveniences itself. It indebts itself.

When Jesus concludes the story, he asks the legal expert, "Which of these proved to be his neighbor?" The stately Jewish man almost chokes on his answer. He can't quite bring himself to say, "The Samaritan." All he can say is, "The one who showed him mercy."

Jewish hatred toward the Samaritans was both racial and religious. Samaritans were half-breeds, being a mixture of Jewish and Assyrian blood, and from the Jews' perspective they were heretics.

They worshiped at a temple on Mount Gerazim, in defiance to the Jewish temple in Jerusalem. They accepted only the first five books of the Bible as their sacred scripture, rather than the entire Jewish Old Testament. They established their own priesthood, independent from the one the Jews had, and they disregarded the traditions of the Jewish elders.

Knowing Jewish sentiment toward Samaritans, can you imagine how hard it must have been for that Jewish legal expert to have the central commandment in Jewish Law illustrated to him by a man whose race he utterly despised?

Just a chapter earlier in Luke's gospel, an entire Samaritan village rejected Jesus. "And he sent messengers on ahead. They went into a Samaritan village to get things ready for him, but the people there did not

℘

welcome him, because he was heading for Jerusalem. When the disciples James and John saw this, they asked, 'Lord, do you want us to call fire down from heaven to destroy them?' But Jesus turned and rebuked them, and they went to another village."

Knowing that Jesus was a Jew and realizing his recent rejection by the Samaritans, you would think he would have cast the Samaritan in the role of the man who fell among thieves. Or worse, as one of the men who turned away.

But Jesus didn't do that. He made the Samaritan the hero of his story.

The hero.

When his disciples wanted to curse the Samaritans for their unneighborly attitude, Jesus blessed them instead by using one of them as an example of everything a good neighbor should be.

Giving a blessing in place of a curse.

That is how the Savior lived. That is how he died. And maybe, in the final analysis, that is the most instructive thing about this parable.

PRAYER

ear Jesus,

Why is it you so often place religious leaders in such a bad light? Help me to understand that, Lord. And help me to see that reflected in that light, however dimly, is an image of myself.

As I have traveled down the road to my many responsibilities, how often have I taken a detour around the person in need? How often have I dismissed that need as none of my business?

Forgive me, Lord, for being so concerned about my other commitments that I am unconcerned about my commitment to others. Help me to realize that so much of true ministry is not what I schedule but what comes as an intrusion to my schedule.

Keep my schedule flexible enough, Lord, so that when my path comes across someone in need, I would be quick to change my plans in preference to yours.

Give me a heart of compassion that I may love my neighbor the way the good Samaritan loved his. Give me eyes that do not look away and feet that do not turn to the other side of the road.

Who is my neighbor, Lord?

> Is it the shut-in, stripped of her indepen-
> dence by arthritis, beaten down by the
> years, hanging on to life by a thread?
> Is it the AIDS victim, stripped of a long
> life, battered by an insidious virus, his

life silently flickering away unnoticed in a hospice?

Is it the bag lady, stripped of her home, broken by the hard reality of the pavement, kept alive by the pocket change of a few kind strangers?

Is it the old man on the street, stripped of his dignity, beaten down by alcohol, half-starved as he rummages through a dumpster for his daily bread?

Is it the woman next door, stripped of her happiness, black and blue from a bad marriage, wishing she were dead?

Is it the man down the hall, stripped of his assets, battered by the economy, whose business is bankrupt?

Deep down inside, Lord, my heart knows the answer. I don't even have to ask. These are my neighbors.

Help me to love them.

Deliver me from stillborn emotions, which look at those on the roadside with a tear in my eye but without the least intention of helping them. Impress upon my heart, Lord, that the smallest act of kindness is better than the greatest of kind intentions.

Help me to realize that although I cannot do everything to alleviate the suffering in this world, I can do something. And even if that something is a very little thing, it is better than turning my head and walking away. . . .

ॐ

AN
INSTRUCTIVE MOMENT
ABOUT LIFE

❧

SCRIPTURE

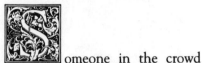 omeone in the crowd said to him, "Teacher, tell my brother to divide the inheritance with me."

Jesus replied, "Man, who appointed me a judge or an arbiter between you?" Then he said to them, "Watch out! Be on your guard against all kinds of greed; a man's life does not consist in the abundance of his possessions."

And he told them this parable:

"The ground of a certain rich man produced a good crop. He thought to himself, 'What shall I do? I have no place to store my crops.'

"Then he said, 'This is what I'll do. I will tear down my barns and build bigger ones, and there I will store all my grain and my goods. And I'll say to myself, "You have plenty of good things laid up for many years. Take life easy; eat, drink and be merry." '

"But God said to him, 'You fool! This very night your life will be demanded from you. Then who will get what you have prepared for yourself?'

"This is how it will be with anyone who stores things up for himself but is not rich toward God."

Luke 12:13–21

℘

MEDITATION

t is a comic scene or a tragic one, depending on how you look at it.

Jesus is speaking to a standing-room-only crowd. Luke tells us earlier that thousands are gathered there, craning their necks, cupping their ears, hoping to catch a pearl or two falling from his lips.

Then in the middle of Jesus' sermon, one man bellies up to the front row and blurts out: "Teacher, tell my brother to divide the inheritance." His face is flushed; his voice, anxious and insistent.

The man is so worried he won't get his snout into the feeding trough of his family's estate that nothing else matters to him. Not even social etiquette. He doesn't care about the point Jesus is making or about the people who are gathered to hear it. All he cares about is himself.

But Jesus shoos away the selfish demand: "Man, who appointed me a judge or an arbiter between you?" Without skipping a beat the Savior turns the intrusive moment into an instructive one. "Watch out!" he warns his followers. "Be on your guard against all kinds of greed; a man's life does not consist in the abundance of his possessions."

Jesus illustrates his point with a parable about a rich man.

The man is a farmer. His hands were once calloused from years of working the land. But he is rich now and can pay to put calluses on other people's hands. Still, you can tell by looking at him that his wealth has been hard-earned.

❧

His eyes have a certain squint to them from so much time spent in the hot sun. His weathered face is a fretwork of wrinkles from years of worrying about his crops: Will the rains come early this year? Will the locusts be back? Will the price for grain be stable?

In earlier years he was the first one up in the morning and the last one to bed at night. His days were spent checking over the equipment, overseeing the hired hands, plodding through the furrows of his field for a first-hand look at the condition of his crops. His nights were spent figuring profits by the dim light of an oil lamp, thinking of ways to squeeze a few more bushels out of each day.

But as the years flew by and his barns filled up, the rich man looked forward to the day when he didn't have to depend on the rain or fight off the locusts or worry about the fluctuating price of grain.

That day came with a bumper crop so big his barns couldn't contain it. So he sketched the blueprints for one last building project, and right beside it he unrolled his plans for retirement.

"I will tear down my barns and build bigger ones, and there I will store all my grain and my goods. And I'll say to myself, 'You have plenty of good things laid up for many years. Take life easy; eat, drink and be merry.'"

The rich man is the envy of all his neighbors. In their eyes he is the epitome of hard work and wise planning. But in the eyes of God he is a fool. He has prepared for every harvest except the most important one—the one that would come that night.

Cloaked in darkness, death comes to him without so much as a whisper of warning. And in a sudden grim reaping, the rich man is taken away.

But not one grain of his wealth goes with him.

All that he has stored away for himself is left to be dispersed among his heirs. It will be fought over in the same way that the man in the crowd fought with his brother over the inheritance their father had left.

Such poor estate planning on behalf of the rich man! He had gathered everything in his barns except an understanding of what life was all about.

He failed to understand that life is not about things. Not about how much you accumulate. Not even about enjoying what you've accumulated.

What then is life all about?

When Jesus finishes the parable, he turns to his disciples and answers that question.

> "Therefore I tell you, do not worry about your life, what you will eat; or about your body, what you will wear. Life is more than food, and the body more than clothes. Consider the ravens: They do not sow or reap, they have no storeroom or barn; yet God feeds them. And how much more valuable you are than birds! Who of you by worrying can add a single hour to

༄

his life? Since you cannot do this very little thing, why do you worry about the rest?

"Consider how the lilies grow. They do not labor or spin. Yet I tell you, not even Solomon in all his splendor was dressed like one of these. If that is how God clothes the grass of the field, which is here today, and tomorrow is thrown into the fire, how much more will he clothe you, O you of little faith! And do not set your heart on what you will eat or drink; do not worry about it. For the pagan world runs after all such things, and your Father knows that you need them. But seek his kingdom, and these things will be given to you as well.

"Do not be afraid, little flock, for your Father has been pleased to give you the kingdom. Sell your possessions and give to the poor. Provide purses for yourselves that will not wear out, a treasure in heaven that will not be exhausted, where no thief comes near and no moth destroys. For where your treasure is, there your heart will be also."

Life. It's about more than what is necessary to sustain it. It's about where we put our trust and where we put our treasure. It's about being rich toward God.

Sad that the rich man couldn't have been in that crowd to hear that investment advice. And ironic that a

❧

man whose life was lived so close to the soil was so deaf to the parables God had hidden there.

Had the rich man not heard the message of the wildflowers that blossomed on his farm and then withered away? "All men are like grass, and all their glory is like the flowers of the field." Had he thought his glory would somehow escape that fate and bloom eternal?

Maybe if he had been less preoccupied with looking after himself, he might have heard the parables preached to him by the lilies of the field and the ravens of the air. Lilies that grew right under his feet. Ravens that hovered right above his head.

Those few instructive moments with the Savior fell on thousands of ears. But only a few really heard. And the one who heard least was the man who worried most—the man who interrupted Jesus in the middle of his sermon.

Such comedy. Such tragedy.

He worried about getting a portion of an estate when an entire kingdom was offered to him. A pearl of great price placed right under his nose, and he was frantically snuffling around for a few kernels of leftover corn.

PRAYER

ear Teacher,

Teach me what life is all about.

Help me to learn that it does not consist of possessions, no matter how many, no matter how nice.

Help me to realize that the more things I selfishly accumulate, the more barns I will have to build to store them in. Help me to realize, too, that the storage fee on such things is subtracted from a life that could be rich toward you instead.

Where have I enriched myself at the expense of my soul? Where have I been a fool? Show me, Lord. While there is still time to change.

Teach me that life is more than the things necessary to sustain it. Help me to learn that if life is more than food, surely it is more important than how the dining room looks; if it's more than clothes, certainly it is more important than whether there's enough closet space to hold them.

Keep me from treasuring those things, Lord. I don't want my heart to be stored up in some cupboard or closet the way that rich man's heart was stored up in his barns. I want my heart to be with you, treasuring the things you treasure.

Show me what those things are, Lord.

Sweep my heart clean of every kind of greed. Empty my closets for those who need clothes, and my cupboards for those who don't know where their next meal is coming from.

Help me to realize that just as I brought nothing into this world, so I can take nothing out, and that the only riches I will have in heaven are those which have gone before me, the riches which I have placed in the hands of the poor for your safekeeping. . . .

AN
INSTRUCTIVE MOMENT
ABOUT HUMILITY

&

SCRIPTURE

o some who were con-
fident of their own righteousness and looked down on
everybody else, Jesus told this parable:

"Two men went up to the temple to pray, one a
Pharisee and the other a tax collector. The Pharisee stood
up and prayed about himself; 'God, I thank you that I am
not like other men—robbers, evildoers, adulterers—or
even like this tax collector. I fast twice a week and give a
tenth of all I get.'"

"But the tax collector stood at a distance. He would
not even look up to heaven, but beat his breast and said,
'God, have mercy on me, a sinner.'

"I tell you that this man, rather than the other, went
home justified before God. For everyone who exalts
himself will be humbled, and he who humbles himself
will be exalted."

Luke 18:9–14

MEDITATION

ax collectors are the
dung on the sandals of the Jewish community. The
stench is particularly repugnant to Jewish nostrils because
the tax collectors are fellow Jews.

Licensed by the Roman government, they put tolls on
roads, tariffs on imports, and taxes on anything they can
get away with. Every time you turn around they have
their hands in your pockets. And if you resist, they resort
to force or threaten to turn you over to the Romans.

It's understandable, then, why the Jews detest any
contact with them. Understandable, too, why it furrowed
a few brows when Jesus reached into this mound of dung
to mold one of his disciples.

> Jesus went out and saw a tax collector
> by the name of Levi sitting at his tax
> booth. "Follow me," Jesus said to him, and
> Levi got up, left everything and followed
> him.
> Then Levi held a great banquet for
> Jesus at his house, and a large crowd of tax
> collectors and others were eating with
> them. But the Pharisees and the teachers of
> the law who belonged to their sect com-
> plained to his disciples, "Why do you eat
> and drink with tax collectors and 'sin-
> ners'?"

Didn't Jesus know that you can't walk through a
pigpen without getting manure on your sandals? He
should have been scraping these people off his feet, but
instead he sat next to them at their dinner table, eating

≈

and drinking and—God help him—enjoying their company. Why? What was it about the riff-raff that attracted him?

"It is not the healthy who need a doctor," Jesus explained, "but the sick. I have not come to call the righteous, but sinners to repentance."

That call was heard by one of the tax collectors sitting at Levi's table. It troubled him all night, and it kept troubling him all the next morning. By noon he couldn't take it anymore, and he responded to the call.

That hour happens to be an hour of prayer, one of the appointed times when every devout Jew goes to the temple to pray. A steady stream of petitioners flows through the western gate, past the outer courtyard of the Gentiles, and into the inner courtyard of the Israelites. The tax collector finds himself caught in a current of that stream and is swept along with them.

Once he is inside the temple grounds, his steps grow timid. This is unfamiliar ground to him, this holy ground. The noonday sun makes him even more self-conscious, and he retreats to the shadows of the marble columns bordering the courtyard.

In the safety of those shadows his eyes pool. His head falls forward, and remorse spills from his soul to spot the stone floor beneath him.

A Pharisee also comes this hour to pray. He comes every day at each of the four appointed hours of prayer. He stops and takes his position somewhere in the center of the courtyard, his usual spot.

❧

As he prays, he looks neither upward in worship nor downward in remorse but sideways in comparison to the others who have gathered there. His eyes skim the scrawl of sins written so legibly across their faces. He is pleased with the comparison.

> "God, I thank you that I am not like other men—robbers, evildoers, adulterers —or even like this tax collector. I fast twice a week and give a tenth of all I get."

The Pharisee's posture is erect. He is proud he has stood resolute against the temptations that have ruined lesser men. And he is proud he has stood as an example to others. He fasts twice a week, which is above the requirements of the Law. He gives a tenth of all his income, which is beyond the practices of his peers.

Taking inventory, the Pharisee is satisfied with the account of his life. The tax collector, however, is not.

> "God, have mercy on me, a sinner."

He stands in the distance, sobbing. He is painfully aware of the sins levied against him, but he is too ashamed to list them. He knows the greed. He knows the deceit. He knows the ledger of injustices credited to his account.

That's why his eyes are downcast. That's why he beats his fists against his chest. And that's why he stands in a corner of the courtyard; his only companions, the shadows cast by columns of cool and indifferent stone.

But God sees the tax collector slumped in those

shadows. His heart overflows with mercy for the man, and his eyes glisten with approval.

In that same city a couple of generations later when the esteemed teacher rabbi Eliezer ben Hyrcanus was on his deathbed, his disciples asked him to teach them the ways of life. His last words to them were: "When you pray, realize before whom you stand."

In that courtyard at that hour of prayer, both the Pharisee and the tax collector realized *where* they stood.

Only one of them realized before *whom*.

That is what humbled the tax collector. And that is what lifted him from being the dung on everybody's sandals to become the delight in the eyes of the Almighty.

PRAYER

od,

Have mercy on me, a sinner. . . .

☙

An
INSTRUCTIVE MOMENT
ABOUT FORGIVENESS

℀

ow one of the Pharisees invited Jesus to have dinner with him, so he went to the Pharisee's house and reclined at the table. When a woman who had lived a sinful life in that town learned that Jesus was eating at the Pharisee's house, she brought an alabaster jar of perfume, and as she stood behind him at his feet weeping, she began to wet his feet with her tears. Then she wiped them with her hair, kissed them and poured perfume on them.

When the Pharisee who had invited him saw this, he said to himself, "If this man were a prophet, he would know who is touching him and what kind of woman she is—that she is a sinner."

Jesus answered him, "Simon, I have something to tell you."

"Tell me, teacher," he said.

"Two men owed money to a certain moneylender. One owed him five hundred denarii, and the other fifty. Neither of them had the money to pay him back, so he canceled the debts of both. Now which of them will love him more?"

Simon replied, "I suppose the one who had the bigger debt canceled."

"You have judged correctly," Jesus said.

Then he turned toward the woman and said to Simon, "Do you see this woman? I came into your house. You did not give me any water for my feet, but she wet my feet with her tears and wiped them with her hair. You did not give me a kiss, but this woman, from the time I entered, has not stopped kissing my feet. You did not put oil on my head, but she has poured perfume on my feet. Therefore, I tell you, her many sins have been forgiven— for she loved much. But he who has been forgiven little loves little."

Then Jesus said to her, "Your sins are forgiven."

The other guests began to say among themselves, "Who is this who even forgives sins?"

Jesus said to the woman, "Your faith has saved you; go in peace."

Luke 7:36–50

ઙ

MEDITATION

he is a prostitute. Her evenings are spent standing on a street corner, soliciting business; her mornings are spent sleeping in, nursing hangovers.

She drinks with her lovers to get her through the evening. She drinks alone when they have gone. Until at last she drinks herself to sleep. For her, the wine isn't a beverage; it's a painkiller. It makes her numb. And numb is the best she can hope to feel.

It is dusk and once again she pours herself a drink. She lies a moment on her bed and stares at the ceiling, her thoughts mingling with the aromatic spices that are pressed between the layers of her sheets.

How many times has she lain there with a man, staring at that same ceiling, pretending to enjoy herself, pretending she was not only wanted but needed and—in her wildest of fantasies—loved?

But she realizes she was wanted for only one thing, needed for only a night, and loved not at all.

She sighs as she gets up to get ready for still another night. Around her neck she puts a necklace from which hangs a small, alabaster jar of perfume. She fixes her hair seductively, drapes a few tawdry scarves around her shoulders, smears some color onto her face, and puts on a pair of spangled earrings.

She goes out to her customary corner, where she takes the vial of perfume and dabs a little on her neck. She has met all manner of men on that corner, from shopkeepers to those who tax them to those who receive their tithes.

They want to stay with her at night, but by morning they are gone. Men. They're all alike.

Or so she thinks until she meets Jesus.

She meets him on his way to a dinner engagement. As he approaches her corner, she counts on her perfume to lure him. In case it doesn't, she brushes a hand against her earrings to catch his eye.

But his eyes do not follow the contours of her body. Instead, they look beneath the spangles and the scarves to see what it is that brings her to this street corner night after night.

She feels his eyes pressed hard against the hollow contours of her soul, and in uncharacteristic modesty, she pulls a scarf over her face.

He speaks to her, and in a moment she realizes he must be a prophet. How else could he discern her silent shame? How else could he know her secret longings?

He tells her that the love she longs for is not on that street corner. He tells her about a love so pure it can wash away all her sin, no matter how unsightly the stain or how permanent it may seem on the surface. It is the love of God. And it is hers for the asking.

She listens in veiled silence. After a few more words Jesus leaves for his appointment. In his absence she drops her veil. A spade of conscience digs at her heart. She gropes for her chest, but all she feels is the cold alabaster jar nestled in her bosom.

The thought that anyone could love her like that—

&

let alone God—overpowers her. She falls to her knees, pleading for this forgiveness, begging to know this love.

She gets up, disoriented, and runs down the street. She accosts people to ask if they have seen Jesus, if they know where he went. She scours the streets, the alleyways, but the night seems to have enveloped him. After an anxious half hour of searching, she finds someone who thinks he saw Jesus go into Simon's house.

She arrives at the Pharisee's house, breathless, her heart beating against her ribs like a suddenly caged bird.

From the open doorway she sees soft mats bordering a low table where guests are reclining, propped on their elbows. The servants are busy filling goblets and replenishing trays of food, so she's able to slip into the room unnoticed.

She approaches the table reverently and stops at the feet of him who is now her Savior.

Suddenly, everybody's attention turns to her: "Look what the cat dragged in" . . . "A sinner in Simon's house?" . . . "This ought to be interesting."

Self-consciously she clutches the small alabaster jar dangling from her neck, then collapses, sobbing in a heap of scarves. She buries her face in the Savior's feet, showering them with the love that spills from her eyes.

Simon sits up. The moment is awkward for the host. He knows the woman's reputation. If Jesus were a prophet, he reasons, he would know too. And if Jesus

❧

were a righteous man, he would certainly send her away with a good scolding.

But Jesus neither scolds her nor sends her away.

Wiping her eyes, the woman sees the mess her tears have made as they've mixed with the dust on his feet. She untresses her hair to clean them and to dry them. As she does, she kisses them.

Hair that was once used to seduce is now used to serve. Kisses that were once for sale are now freely given away.

Then, as if to cleanse Jesus of her unworthy kisses, she opens her vial of perfume and pours the sweet fragrance over his feet.

The scent fills the room and thoughts run through Simon's mind so fast they almost trip over themselves. *How scandalous. How can Jesus let her carry on that way? Doesn't he know who she is?*

Jesus proves himself to be a prophet, not by discerning the morals of the woman but by discerning the mind of the host. He clears up the confusion in Simon's mind with a parable.

"Two men owed money to a certain moneylender. One owed him five hundred denarii, and the other fifty. Neither of them had the money to pay him back, so he canceled the debts of both. Now which of them will love him more?"

"I suppose," concedes the Pharisee with some reluctance, "the one who had the bigger debt canceled."

&

But the debt Jesus calls into account is not the prostitute's; it's the Pharisee's.

"I came into your house. You did not give me any water for my feet, but she wet my feet with her tears and wiped them with her hair. You did not give me a kiss, but this woman, from the time I entered, has not stopped kissing my feet. You did not put oil on my head, but she has poured perfume on my feet."

The forgiveness that has been lavished on this woman is evidenced by the love she has lavished on Jesus. Tears, hair, kisses, perfume. Tokens of her love. Testimonies of her forgiveness.

This woman of the night found in the Savior what she could never find on that street corner. Forgiveness for her sins. Salvation for her soul. Peace for her heart. And the love she so desperately longed for. Love that would be with her not just for the night . . . but forever.

PRAYER

ear Lord,

Forgive me for all the ways I have prostituted my life. For how I have attracted attention to myself. For how I have compromised my character. For how I have cheapened my life and the lives of others.

My debt is great, O Lord.

Forgive me for all the times I have been pharisaical. For when I have judged someone's heart by the clothes they have had on. For when I have looked down on someone who was worshiping you in a way that was different from my way. For all the tearless times I have entertained your presence.

My debt is great, O Lord.

Forgive me the sins I have committed, which, like the prostitute's, are many. Forgive me the opportunities to serve you that I have neglected, which, like the Pharisee's, are also many.

My debt is great, O Lord.

Help me to realize the extent of that debt so I may appreciate the extent of your graciousness in canceling it, and love you all the more. . . .

AN
INSTRUCTIVE MOMENT
ABOUT OUR FATHER

&

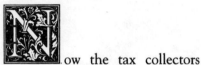ow the tax collectors and "sinners" were all gathering around to hear him. But the Pharisees and the teachers of the law muttered, "This man welcomes sinners and eats with them."

Then Jesus told them this parable: . . .

"There was a man who had two sons. The younger one said to his father, 'Father, give me my share of the estate.' So he divided his property between them.

"Not long after that, the younger son got together all he had, set off for a distant country and there squandered his wealth in wild living. After he had spent everything, there was a severe famine in that whole country, and he began to be in need. So he went and hired himself out to a citizen of that country, who sent him to his fields to feed pigs. He longed to fill his stomach with the pods that the pigs were eating, but no one gave him anything.

"When he came to his senses, he said, 'How many of my father's hired men have food to spare, and here I am starving to death! I will set out and go back to my father and say to him: Father, I have sinned against heaven and against you. I am no longer worthy to be called your son; make me like one of your hired men.' So he got up and went to his father.

"But while he was still a long way off, his father saw him and was filled with compassion for him; he ran to his son, threw his arms around him and kissed him.

"The son said to him, 'Father, I have sinned against heaven and against you. I am no longer worthy to be called your son.'

"But the father said to his servants, 'Quick! Bring the best robe and put it on him. Put a ring on his finger and sandals on his feet. Bring the fattened calf and kill it. Let's have a feast and celebrate. For this son of mine was dead and is alive again; he was lost and is found.' So they began to celebrate.

"Meanwhile, the older son was in the field. When he came near the house, he heard music and dancing. So he called one of the servants and asked what was going on. 'Your brother has come,' he replied, 'and your father has killed the fattened calf because he has him back safe and sound.'

"The older brother became angry and refused to go in. So his father went out and pleaded with him. But he answered his father, 'Look! All these years I've been slaving for you and never disobeyed your orders. Yet you never gave me even a young goat so I could celebrate with my friends. But when this son of yours who has squandered your property with prostitutes comes home, you kill the fattened calf for him!'

" 'My son,' the father said, 'you are always with me, and everything I have is yours. But we had to celebrate and be glad, because this brother of yours was dead and is alive again; he was lost and is found.' "

Luke 15:1–3, 11–32

MEDITATION

he word *Pharisee* means "separated one." The Pharisees were a strict, conservative sect who separated themselves not only from any contact with Gentiles and sinful Jews but even from religious Jews who were less devout than they were.

For the Pharisee, purity was an obsession. Doctrinal purity. Moral purity. Ceremonial purity. Racial purity. Social purity. It affected every area of their lives—from the way they prepared their food to the way they washed their hands before they ate it to the people they sat down to eat it with.

To them, sharing a meal with a sinner or tax collector would not only be a defilement but a tacit acceptance of that lifestyle.

"How could Jesus do such a thing?" the Pharisees murmured to themselves. "How could he tolerate those people touching him, crowding around him, and worse, eating with him? Doesn't he care about purity? Has he no regard for the tradition of the elders? What kind of example is he setting? What kind of message is he sending?"

When Jesus hears their murmurings, he strings together three parables to illustrate why he enjoys the company of sinners. The parables are arranged climactically. A lost sheep. A lost coin. A lost son. In the final parable Jesus casts these religious separatists as a key character in his story.

Why the younger son in the parable wants to leave home, we are not told. Maybe it's because he's had enough of his straight-laced brother. Enough of his critical attitude. Enough of his condescending looks. Enough of his carping remarks.

Maybe he feels he can never measure up, never be in his father's eyes what his older brother is.

Maybe he feels saddled with too much responsibility, cinched tight by all the chores that are necessary in running a farm.

Or maybe his passions are champing at the bit, and he resents his father's reins holding them back. Maybe he's wanting some open pasture so those passions can run free.

For whatever reason, he wants out.

"Father, give me my share of the estate."

How it must have crushed the father to hear those words.

But just as God did not fence off the forbidden tree from Adam and Eve, so this father does not restrain his son from the lush temptations hanging on the boughs of the distant country. He lets him go, hoping, all the while, that the road which leads away from home will be the very road that someday brings him back.

As the son crests that last hill and disappears over the horizon, the father breaks down and weeps. But his son doesn't see those tears. He's off to see the world, and he isn't looking back.

He takes with him a bag of money and finds a quick circle of friends who are eager to help him spend it. He

&

eats all the food he wants, drinks all the wine he wants, indulges himself with all the women he wants. And he has no responsibility except to pay the tab at the end of the evening.

He is determined to taste every fruit, however forbidden, that life has to offer. And he is determined to put home as far out of his mind as he can.

But although the son has forgotten his father, his father has not forgotten him. Every meal the vacant place at the table reminds him of his missing son. Every time he passes the empty bedroom, a torrent of memories washes over him. Every time he sees his one son, it reminds him of the other son he would not see. Maybe ever.

As for that son, the party continues. Night after raucous night. Until one morning he wakes up with more than a hangover. One morning the money runs out. And so do his friends. A famine then sweeps across the land, and suddenly he finds himself down and out in a distant country, far from the happiness he thought he would find there.

He tramps from door to door, begging for work. But he is a penniless transient now, and the only work he can get is a job slopping pigs.

So great is the famine that the pigs are more valuable than the people who care for them. His cheeks are drawn. His eyes are hollow. His skin is sucked in around his ribs. He is ready to get on his hands and knees to feed with the pigs when he finally comes to his senses.

What brings him to his senses is a picture of home—a

&

picture of how well his father provided for the lowliest of his hired help. That picture is what caused him to turn his back on the distant country and take the long walk home. Maybe he could hire on as one of his father's servants. The work would be hard, he knows, but with three meals a day, at least he'd have the strength to do it.

As the son is on his way home, the father is on his knees. How many tears has he shed? How many sleepless nights has he spent? How many hours during the day has he wondered about his son's whereabouts, worried about his safety, wished for his return? How many times has he sat on his porch at the end of a day, reading the horizon as if it were a line from a psalm of lament, searching for some word of hope?

One late afternoon as the father is studying that horizon, a dot suddenly punctuates it. He squints (his eyes are not what they used to be), and the dot becomes more distinct. He follows it down the sloping road until at last he recognizes the familiar stride. It's wearier than he remembers, but it's the stride of his son! And a rush of emotion sends him running.

As the father draws near, he sees a haggard vestige of the person who left home so long ago. The son is unkempt, faint from hunger, and his spindly legs barely support him. But with what little strength he has, he rehearses his scripted confession one more time.

When the father finally reaches him, he doesn't make him grovel in the dirt. He doesn't question him to make sure he's learned his lesson. And he doesn't lecture him: "Look at you, you're a disgrace" . . . "I knew when the

☙

money ran out that you'd come crawling back" . . . "You can come home, but only on one condition."

The father says none of those things.

Instead he throws his arms around the son's neck and showers him with kisses, tears rushing from his eyes in a riptide of emotion. The son tries to recite his carefully worded confession, but the father hears none of it. It's not important.

It is enough that his son is alive and that he has come home.

For the son's lost dignity, the father bestows on him a robe of honor. For his bare servant's feet, he puts on them the sandals of a son. For the hand that squandered an entire inheritance, he gives a signet ring that reinstates the son's position of authority in the family business. For his empty stomach, he hosts a feast fit for a king.

A robe, a pair of sandals, a ring, a feast. Symbols not only of forgiveness but of restoration. Gifts of grace, lavished on the one who deserved them least.

Enter the older brother—the dutiful older brother who doesn't have a delinquent bone in his body—and suddenly a flat note sounds in the celebration. He is incensed by the festivities and refuses to join in.

At this point in the telling of the story, the Pharisees and teachers of the law see themselves cast in the role of the older brother. But they are deaf to the fact that their character is a tragic one. Their ears hear only the righteous indignation of the older brother, not the heartfelt call of the father.

The father's words are not authoritarian but rather ones of affection. "My son, you are always with me and everything I have is yours. But we had to celebrate and be glad, because this brother of yours was dead and is alive again; he was lost and is found."

The parable reveals the joy in heaven when just one lost person finds his way into the Father's arms. But it reveals more than that.

Jesus said, "No man knows who the Father is except the Son and those to whom the Son chooses to reveal him."

In the parable, Jesus shows us an example of everything an earthly father was meant to be: tender, compassionate, understanding, demonstrative in his love. But he shows us something else. He cracks the door to heaven, ever so slightly, to reveal his own Father.

Through that slender opening we see a purity that the Pharisees couldn't seem to understand. The purity of a father's love. A love that didn't play favorites. A love that reached out not only to the prodigal, lost in a distant country . . . but to the pharisaical, lost just outside the doorstep of home.

PRAYER

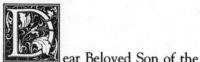ear Beloved Son of the
Father, how it must crush you when I turn my back on
you and walk away. How you must weep when you see me
disappear over a far horizon to squander my life in a
distant country.

Thank you that although I have sometimes left home,
I have never left your heart. Though I have forgotten
about you, you have never forgotten about me.

Thank you for the financial crisis or the famine or the
pigsty or whatever it took to bring me to my senses. And
thank you that even though what brought me home were
pangs of hunger instead of pangs of conscience, yet still,
even on those terms you welcomed me back.

Thank you for the forgiveness and the restoration you
have lavished upon me—me, the one who needed them
most but deserved them least.

I confess that there is inside me not only a prodigal
son but also a critical older brother.

How dutiful I have sometimes been, and yet so proud
of the duties I have done. How generous I have been in
my opinion of myself, and yet so judgmental in my
opinion of others. How often I have entered into
criticism, and yet how seldom I have entered into your
joy.

Gather both the prodigal part of myself and the
critical part of myself in your loving arms, O Lord. And
bring them home. . . .

AN
INSTRUCTIVE MOMENT
ABOUT PRAYER

&

SCRIPTURE

ne day Jesus was pray-
ing in a certain place. When he finished, one of his
disciples said to him, "Lord, teach us to pray, just as John
taught his disciples."

He said to them, "When you pray, say:

" 'Father,
hallowed be your name,
your kingdom come.
Give us each day
our daily bread.
Forgive us our sins,
for we also forgive
everyone who sins against us.
And lead us not into temptation.' "

Then he said to them, "Suppose one of you has a
friend, and he goes to him at midnight and says, 'Friend,
lend me three loaves of bread, because a friend of mine
on a journey has come to me, and I have nothing to set
before him.'

"Then the one inside answers, 'Don't bother me. The
door is already locked, and my children are with me in
bed. I can't get up and give you anything.' I tell you,
though he will not get up and give him the bread because
he is his friend, yet because of the man's boldness he will
get up and give him as much as he needs.

"So I say to you: Ask and it will be given to you; seek
and you will find; knock and the door will be opened to
you. For everyone who asks receives; he who seeks finds;
and to him who knocks, the door will be opened.

℥

"Which of you fathers, if your son asks for a fish, will give him a snake instead? Or if he asks for an egg, will give him a scorpion? If you then, though you are evil, know how to give good gifts to your children, how much more will your Father in heaven give the Holy Spirit to those who ask him!"

Luke 11:1–13

MEDITATION

he disciples were just children, really.

"Follow me," Jesus said, "and I will make you fishers of men." And immediately the disciples dropped their nets and followed him.

Who, other than children, would so recklessly abandon the responsibilities of adult life for such a swashbuckling promise of adventure?

Following Jesus was like falling into a fairy tale. Water turned into wine. Thousands fed from a boy's lunch box. A stormy sea suddenly calmed. A blind man healed. A demon-possessed man delivered. A dead child brought back to life.

The disciples were as wide-eyed as children in Wonderland. Always popping up their hands with questions. Ever eager to learn.

"Lord, teach us to pray."

The disciples had seen Jesus pray on many occasions. Sometimes they would awake stiffly in the middle of the night to find him absent from the weary band of men huddled in fetal warmth around the gray embers of the campfire. He would be off somewhere by himself, praying. And occasionally, in the quiet of night, they could overhear him.

His prayers were not a filigree of golden words as were the prayers of the religious leaders they were so accustomed to hearing. Neither were they the ecstatic bab-

ℰ

blings heard coming from the pagan temples. They had the familiar warmth of a son speaking to his father.

The disciples yearned for that type of intimacy with God, but they didn't know how to attain it.

"Lord, teach us to pray, just as John taught his disciples."

So Jesus sits down and teaches them. The lesson is less what you'd expect to find on a seminary student's shelf and more what you'd expect to find framed above a child's bed. An embroidered sampler maybe. With a stitchwork angel off to one side, kneeling with a child in prayer:

> 'Father,
> hallowed be your name,
> your kingdom come.
> Give us each day
>   our daily bread.
> Forgive us our sins,
>   for we also forgive
>   everyone who sins against us.
> And lead us not into temptation.'"

So childlike the approach. So simple the requests. In that unpretentious prayer we are asked to bring to God our hopes for the future as well as the hunger we have right now; we are asked to bring yesterday's failures as well as tomorrow's fears.

When we do, God will not turn us away. However, like a good father, he thoughtfully considers our requests before answering them. During that time we often fidget as we wait, just like children. In our impatience there is the danger of distorting both our needs and his response to them.

When our needs are desperate, we become like the man with the bare cupboards in the parable whose traveling friend dropped in on him unexpectedly. Frantically we run to God, but in seeking him we feel only the chilly aloneness of dark and deserted streets. We come to heaven's door, but it seems bolted from the inside. We knock, but we feel we are rousing God from his sleep. We call out to him for help, but all we hear is the muffle of a brusque refusal. So we knock harder and call out louder. And when the door finally does open, we feel as if God has come to our aid begrudgingly.

That is a distorted picture of God and how he responds to our prayers. Look at the parable again.

"Don't bother me," the irritated friend says. "The door is already locked, and my children are with me in bed. I can't get up and give you anything."

Did you see it? Look closer. Snuggled up next to that man are his children. Imagine how differently he would have responded to one of his own children waking up in the middle of the night, saying, "I'm thirsty, Daddy." Or if the children woke up the next morning, saying, "I'm hungry, Daddy." Would he roll over and go back to sleep? No. He would get up and get them what they needed.

The ultimate point of the parable is not persistence; it is to clarify our relationship with God. We are not the frantic friend on the outside, knocking on the door; we are the beloved children on the inside, snuggled next to their father. If a sleeping friend can be roused to meet the needs of another friend in the middle of the night, how much more can a loving father be counted on to come to the aid of his children.

Knowing that makes a big difference in how we pray.

We don't need to beat down the door to get God's attention. All we have to do is whisper. He is that near to us.

And we are that dear to him.

That is why, when the disciples asked Jesus to teach them the ABCs of prayer, he started off the first lesson with the words . . . "Our Father."

PRAYER

ord,

Teach me to pray.

Teach me to come to you with the outstretched arms of a child who runs to its father for comfort. As I come, fill me with all the love, all the respect, all the honor that a child should have for a parent.

Take my small clumsy hands in yours and walk with me, Lord. Lead the way through the dark streets. And help me to keep pace with you so that your will would be done in my life here on earth as it is in heaven.

Deliver me from my childish Christmas list of material prayers. Give me instead what I need this day to sustain my life: both the food I need for my body and the forgiveness I so desperately need for my soul.

I am just a kid in this candystore world, Lord. Remember how weak I am. And please, don't lead me down any aisles where I might become tempted to stray from you. . . .

An
INSTRUCTIVE MOMENT
ABOUT DEATH

&

SCRIPTURE

here was a rich man who was dressed in purple and fine linen and lived in luxury every day. At his gate was laid a beggar named Lazarus, covered with sores and longing to eat what fell from the rich man's table. Even the dogs came and licked his sores.

"The time came when the beggar died and the angels carried him to Abraham's side. The rich man also died and was buried. In hell, where he was in torment, he looked up and saw Abraham far away, with Lazarus by his side. So he called to him, 'Father Abraham, have pity on me and send Lazarus to dip the tip of his finger in water and cool my tongue, because I am in agony in this fire.'

"But Abraham replied, 'Son, remember that in your lifetime you received your good things, while Lazarus received bad things, but now he is comforted here and you are in agony. And besides all this, between us and you a great chasm has been fixed, so that those who want to go from here to you cannot, nor can anyone cross over from there to us.'

"He answered, 'Then I beg you, father, send Lazarus to my father's house, for I have five brothers. Let him warn them, so that they will not also come to this place of torment.'

"Abraham replied, 'They have Moses and the Prophets; let them listen to them.'

"'No, father Abraham,' he said, 'but if someone from the dead goes to them, they will repent.'

&

"He said to them, 'If they do not listen to Moses and the Prophets, they will not be convinced even if someone rises from the dead.'"

Luke 16:19–31

MEDITATION

efore Jesus spoke this
parable, he told an audience of Pharisees that no servant
could serve two masters, that they could not serve both
God and Money, that the divided loyalties would
eventually lead to divided love, causing them to embrace
the one and turn their backs on the other.

But the Pharisees loved money, and when they heard
this, they turned their backs on Jesus and sneered.

Jesus says to them: "You are the ones who justify
yourselves in the eyes of men, but God knows your
hearts. What is highly valued among men is detestable in
God's sight."

And what is highly valued among men is the life the
Pharisees lived—a life of luxury.

The rich man in the parable has such a life. He wears
the finest clothes; robes of purple made from costly Tyrian
dye, expensive linens imported from Egypt.

His gated estate is the finest in the community. Its
sprawling botanic gardens are meticulously kept by a staff
of full-time gardeners. Inside the palatial home are
priceless works of art, valued as the best collection in the
region. Italian marble floors catch the reflections of the
guests in their sheen.

The guests come from the upper echelons of government, business, and the arts. They are the people who
matter in the community, the people who make things
happen, the elite.

Through this gossipy maze of socialites obsequious

servants weave their way to fill waning goblets of wine or to proffer delectable trays of appetizers. The rich man's table is a smorgasbord of epicurean delights, filled with roasted lamb, an assortment of fowl, a trove of culinary treasures from the sea, the choicest of seasonal fruit and vegetables, select wines from the world's best vineyards, breads and sweetcakes looking like miniature works of art.

And this is how the rich man lives, day in, day out.

Then there is Lazarus. The beggar. Dumped at the rich man's gate like a sack of garbage.

Others brought him there to get him out of their neighborhood and because he is too sick and too weak to bring himself. He looks like a broken marionette, lank and wooden and lying in a heap. His scurvied flesh clings desperately to his bones. Gaping sores ooze all over his body, his skin a sieve where his life leaks out.

Who will stop and help such a miserable man? Who will feed him, who will bathe him, who will clothe him? Who will take him in and give him shelter for the night? Who will hold his hand and listen to the story of his life? Who will comb his hair? Clip his toenails? Clean his sores?

Who?

The only aspiration Lazarus has left in life is that one of the guests might be merciful enough to scrape the spillage off the polished marble floors and bring it to him.

But at the rich man's estate mercy is the one thing that is in short supply. None of the guests want to look at Lazarus, let alone come near him or touch him. The very sight of him turns their stomachs. And if the sight of him doesn't, the stench will.

The only mercy Lazarus receives is from the dogs that gather around him to slather his sores with their tongues. At this point he is too far gone to stop them. He is delirious with fever, his face is in the dirt, and from the corner of his mouth a line of drool seeps to the ground and pools.

The finely attired guests come and go, talking, laughing, all the while averting their gaze, careful not to let it fall on the heap of sores plopped beside the gate. The noise they make is muffled, then goes mute.

Slowly Lazarus turns his head to what he thinks is a dog's nose, nuzzling him. But the tongues of the dogs have become the hands of angels. "We've come to take you home," says one of them and smiles kindly. Lazarus rubs his eyes, and the angels pick him up in their arms and carry him away.

His sores are healed; his suffering, forever behind him.

As smoothly as waking up from sleep, Lazarus is taken from that place of humiliation to a place of honor at the table of Abraham.

Death also comes to the rich man. But there are no angels to bear him away. There is no Abraham to embrace him. For all his endless party of friends the only embrace he receives is from a small plot of freshly shoveled earth.

As Lazarus was once slumped in torment outside the gates of the rich man's estate, the rich man is now outside

&

of heaven's gate, lying in a torment of his own. He pleads for mercy. But not even a finger is lifted on his behalf. Death, it seems, fixes a chasm that even mercy cannot bridge.

Death. It is the most misunderstood part of life. It is not a great sleep but a great awakening. It is that moment when we awake, rub our eyes, and see things at last the way God has seen them all along.

When Jesus finishes the parable, the Pharisees are speechless. Where there were sneers, there is now only silence. For it is *their* life he has indicted with his words; *their* heart he has exposed; *their* self-indulgence.

They are the rich men living in luxury, while the Lazaruses of this world are dying just outside their gates.

The rich man and Lazarus. It is the only parable in which a person is specifically named. And that person is not a high-ranking government official, not a wealthy businessman, not a respected socialite, not a noted religious leader. He is a poor beggar covered with sores.

It is to the rich man's shame—his eternal shame— that he knew that poor beggar's name but wouldn't give him so much as a scrap of food that fell from his table.

But it is to that poor beggar's glory that however miserable his lot in life was, however many of the rich man's guests turned their heads from him, Jesus not only knew him by name but saved a place for him—a place of the highest honor—right next to the founding father of the entire Jewish nation.

&

PRAYER

ear Jesus,

Help me this day to see with the eyes I will one day be given at death. I see clearly enough now what is highly valued in the sight of men. Give me eyes to see what is highly valued in *your* sight.

Is it not the Lazaruses of this world who are lying just outside my gate? Is it not the poor begging for a little something to fall from my table?

Keep me from isolating myself from their sores, Lord. However hard it is to look, make me look.

And when I do, fill my heart with mercy so that if they are hungry I would give them a good hot meal rather than mincing out only enough change for a cup of coffee.

If they are thirsty, help me to give them not just a drink but a few kind words to quench their thirst for a little human kindness.

If they are homeless, help me to give them a night in a hotel or a ride to a homeless shelter or provide someplace safe where they could get a good night's rest.

If they are threadbare, help me to get them some clothes. Clothes that are clean and that fit and that I wouldn't be ashamed of wearing if they were given to me.

If they are sick, help me to nurse them or to pay for a doctor's visit so they can get the help they need.

If they are in prison, help me to give my time in visiting them, my ear in listening to them, and my heart in trying to understand the pain of their isolation and the shame of their imprisonment.

Help me to see, Lord Jesus, that when I do something for the least of these brothers and sisters of the street, I am doing it for you. . . .

AN
INSTRUCTIVE MOMENT
ABOUT GOD'S KINGDOM

SCRIPTURE

On a Sabbath Jesus was teaching in one of the synagogues, and a woman was there who had been crippled by a spirit for eighteen years. She was bent over and could not straighten up at all.

When Jesus saw her, he called her forward and said to her, "Woman, you are set free from your infirmity." Then he put his hands on her, and immediately she straightened up and praised God.

Indignant because Jesus had healed on the Sabbath, the synagogue ruler said to the people, "There are six days for work. So come and be healed on those days, not on the Sabbath."

The Lord answered him, "You hypocrites! Doesn't each of you on the Sabbath untie his ox or donkey from the stall and lead it out to give it water? Then should not this woman, a daughter of Abraham, whom Satan has kept bound for eighteen long years, be set free on the Sabbath day from what bound her?"

When he said this, all his opponents were humiliated, but the people were delighted with all the wonderful things he was doing.

Then Jesus asked,

"What is the kingdom of God like? What shall I compare it to? It is like a mustard seed, which a man took and planted in his garden. It grew and became a tree, and the birds of the air perched in its branches."

Again he asked, "What shall I compare the kingdom of God to? It is like yeast that a woman took and mixed into a large amount of flour until it worked all through the dough."

Luke 13:10–21

hile teaching in a synagogue, Jesus spies a hunched-over woman in the back row, huddled off to herself. He calls her to come forward, and awkwardly, self-consciously, she shuffles her way to the front.

When Jesus uncinches the burden she has been carrying around for the past eighteen years, a rush of youthful feelings comes over her. She straightens up and sets the stiff, dry atmosphere of the synagogue ablaze. But the synagogue leader is quick to pour water on her impassioned praise to keep it from spreading out of control.

When Jesus lashes out at the hypocritical leader, the rejoicing woman sits down and the crowd becomes suddenly subdued.

Jesus seizes that tense moment of silence to search his mind for an illustration about the kingdom of God. He overlooks images from government, military, and civic life. Instead, with the casual ease of a child gathering wildflowers, he picks an image from the people's own backyards—the image of a man planting a mustard seed in his garden.

The mustard seed was one of the most common herbs in the Middle East, used not only in seasoning but in everyday speech. The phrase "as small as a mustard seed" was a proverbial one. Jesus used it when he said, "If you have faith as small as a mustard seed, you can say to this mountain, 'Move from here to there' and it will move." But in spite of its small seeds, the mustard plant could grow so large that a horse and rider could gallop under its branches.

The point of the parable is that the kingdom of God would come from small and seemingly inconsequential beginnings.

Jesus could have used the image of a towering pine tree or a spreading oak. Certainly that would have been a more fitting symbol for the stately grandeur of God's kingdom. But the pine cone and the acorn are not small enough seeds for the purposes of his illustration, for his emphasis is not so much on the future greatness of the kingdom as it is on its present insignificance.

That's what the people in the synagogue were seeing that day. They were seeing a mustard seed planted in the soil of that old woman's heart.

For eighteen years she had come and gone, Sabbath after Sabbath, and found a little inconspicuous place in the back to sit down. No one in the leadership of the synagogue paid her any attention. She was not a big donor. She was not a person on their list to be groomed for any kind of public ministry. She was just a bent-over old woman . . . little more than a mustard seed in the grand scheme of things.

Jesus looks over the synagogue and catches the eye of that woman, sitting erect now, her face moist with tears of joy, and another image comes to his mind to illustrate God's kingdom.

"It is like yeast that a woman took and mixed into a

large amount of flour until it worked all through the dough."

With the back of her hand she wipes away the tears. She knows the illustration is for her. It is Jesus' way of saying that her world matters, too, and that it is brimming with parables of its own.

"The kingdom of God is within you," Jesus once said.

It starts with a little lump of grace hidden within us. And slowly, silently, it permeates our life, lifts it, transforms it.

It worked that way for a tax collector in the temple courtyard. And for a prostitute on the street corner. And for this bent-over woman in the synagogue.

Oddly, Jesus addresses none of the pressing issues that plagued the first century. The government was godless, yet he led no revolt to overthrow it. The populace was heavily taxed, yet he led no rally for economic reform. Many of the people were slaves, yet he led no movement to liberate them. Poverty. Classism. Racism. The list of social ills was as long as it was ugly.

Instead of making that list his political agenda, Jesus was content to plant the tiniest of seeds in the unlikeliest soil, to hide a lump of grace in the life of a nobody.

A fisherman. A tax collector. A centurion.

Heart by heart that's the way the kingdom of God grew. Quietly reaching for the sun. Spreading throughout history so people from every tribe and nation could one day roost in its branches.

A Mary. A Martha. An old woman with a bent-over back.

Expanding, imperceptibly, like a loaf of rising dough . . . and filling the world with the aroma of freshly baked bread.

PRAYER

ear Lord Jesus,

Teach me not to despise small beginnings. For it was in Bethlehem, the least among the cities of Judah, that you chose to start your life on this earth.

Teach me the meaning of little things. For a mere cup of water has eternal significance when given in your name.

Teach me the value of little things. For a widow's mites are the true treasures of heaven.

Teach me to be faithful in little things. For it is by being faithful in little things on this earth that I will be given responsibility for greater things in your kingdom.

Teach me the far-reaching effects of little things. For a simple request by a crucified thief ended up changing his destiny for all eternity.

Teach me the power of little things. For how silently the mustard seed grows, yet how pervasive is its influence; how invisibly the yeast works, yet how transforming is its power. . . .

AN
INSTRUCTIVE MOMENT
ABOUT MERCY

SCRIPTURE

ne Sabbath, when Jesus went to eat in the house of a prominent Pharisee, he was being carefully watched. There in front of him was a man suffering from dropsy. Jesus asked the Pharisees and experts in the law, "Is it lawful to heal on the Sabbath or not?" But they remained silent. So taking hold of the man, he healed him and sent him away.

Then he asked them, "If one of you has a son or an ox that falls into a well on the Sabbath day, will you not immediately pull him out?" And they had nothing to say.

When he noticed how the guests picked the places of honor at the table, he told them this parable:

"When someone invites you to a wedding feast, do not take the place of honor, for a person more distinguished than you may have been invited. If so, the host who invited both of you will come and say to you, 'Give this man your seat.' Then, humiliated, you will have to take the least important place. But when you are invited, take the lowest place, so that when your host comes, he will say to you, 'Friend, move up to a better place.' Then you will be honored in the presence of all your fellow guests. For everyone who exalts himself will be humbled, and he who humbles himself will be exalted."

Then Jesus said to his host, "When you give a luncheon or dinner, do not invite your friends, your brothers or relatives, or your rich neighbors; if you do, they may invite you back, and so you will be repaid. But when you give a banquet, invite the poor, the crippled, the lame, the blind, and you will be blessed. Although they cannot repay you, you will be repaid at the resurrection of the righteous."

When one of those at the table with him heard this, he said to Jesus, "Blessed is the man who will eat at the feast in the kingdom of God."

Jesus replied: "A certain man was preparing a great banquet and invited many guests. At the time of the banquet he sent his servant to tell those who had been invited, 'Come, for everything is now ready.'

"But they all alike began to make excuses. The first said, 'I have just bought a field, and I must go and see it. Please excuse me.'

"Another said, 'I have just bought five yoke of oxen, and I'm on my way to try them out. Please excuse me.'

"Still another said, 'I just got married, so I can't come.'

"The servant came back and reported this to his master. Then the owner of the house became angry and ordered his servant, 'Go out quickly into the streets and alleys of the town and bring in the poor, the crippled, the blind and the lame.'

" 'Sir,' the servant said, 'what you ordered has been done, but there is still room.'

"Then the master told his servant, 'Go out to the roads and country lanes and make them come in, so that my house will be full. I tell you, not one of those men who were invited will get a taste of my banquet.' "

Luke 14:1–24

MEDITATION

igh atop the snow-capped peaks of Mount Hermon, the Jordan River trickles into existence. Fed along the way by tributaries from surrounding mountains, the Jordan flows southward for some two hundred miles, filling the Sea of Galilee, watering the Jordan Valley, and pooling finally into the lowest point on earth, the Dead Sea.

Were it not for that river and its tributaries, Palestine would be a wasteland.

Gazing sleepily over the Jordan Valley, the sun breathes a final Friday afternoon sigh before retiring behind the hills. In a Perean city on the eastern side of the Jordan, shops lining the streets have already closed.

People hurry home to celebrate the Sabbath meal with family and friends, breezing past other people who are in no hurry. People who have no Sabbath in their lives to celebrate. People of the street who have fallen through the cracks of society. People whose lives are ever-widening gullies of hopelessness and despair.

Overlooking those eroding gullies of humanity is the hilltop home of a prominent Pharisee. Jesus has been invited there for dinner. The other guests include a few less prominent Pharisees and a group of legal experts trained in the rigors of Levitical Law.

In keeping with the longstanding custom of eastern hospitality, the door to this dinner party is also open to outsiders. As long as they aren't a distraction, they are welcome to sit around the periphery of the room and listen to the table talk and maybe help dispose of any leftovers.

One of those outsiders is a man with dropsy. The failing pump of his heart has caused his legs to swell, and the excessive fluid makes his movements slow and awkward.

The man is short of breath from trudging up the hill. But he has heard such stories about this Jesus, and if only a fraction of them are true, it would have been well worth the climb. He hobbles toward Jesus, his drop-foot trailing limply behind him. But as he does, he stumbles and falls.

Jesus looks down at the man, then at the legal experts. And he poses a question to see just how well-schooled they really are.

"Is it lawful to heal on the Sabbath or not?"

During their awkward schoolboy silence Jesus takes hold of the man and pulls him up. And by the time the man reaches his feet, he is healed.

Now that Jesus has everybody's attention, he asks another question: "If one of you has a son or an ox that falls into a well on the Sabbath day, will you not immediately pull him out?"

The answer to that question answers the previous one. If you could pull an animal out of a well on the Sabbath, surely you could pull a man out of the valley of suffering he had fallen into. But no one wants to chance being made a fool of in front of such a distinguished group, so no one answers.

Interrupting the awkward moment, the host calls everyone to the table. The men fan out around the U-shaped table. At the head of the table, located at the outer curve of the U, is the place where the most honored guest sits. To the right and left of it are places for the next honored guests, and so forth, in descending order of importance down the table.

While Jesus watches, the dinner guests jockey for position, quick to secure for themselves the places of greatest honor. It would be a humorous scene if it weren't such a pathetic one. Grown men so insecure. So status conscious. So preoccupied with such petty things.

Jesus casually takes the seat that is left and then tells them a parable. He tells them that the lowliest place at the table is not only the safest one from embarrassment but the surest one for advancement. "For everyone who exalts himself will be humbled, and he who humbles himself will be exalted."

But in their petty world, advancement comes by rubbing shoulders with the right people. And you rub shoulders with the right people by securing the right seats at the right banquets. All these right moves, though, add up to something very, very wrong. And Jesus turns to his host to tell him so.

Give banquets for those who need them most, Jesus tells him. For those sentenced to the streets. For those abandoned to the alleyways. For those who can only afford to repay you with a simple "Thank you" or a heartfelt "God bless you."

Sensing Jesus' disapproval of his guest list, the host tenses up. A chasm of silence ensues, which one of the guests tries to bridge by smoothly transitioning the topic of conversation: "Blessed is the man who will eat at the feast in the kingdom of God."

Jesus then turns to the man with the pious platitudes and tells him a parable which reveals the guest list to that feast: those who have been forsaken in the streets; those who have been forgotten in the alleys; and those who have been forced to live on the outer fringes of their society.

Blessed indeed are those who will eat at the feast in the kingdom of God. But it won't be any of the men sitting around the table of the Pharisee. They're too preoccupied with petty things to even hear the invitation.

As we observe the events of that Sabbath evening, we see in the background the landscape of God's kingdom. Look closely. A man with dropsy lies on the floor. A message has been given about how the lowly will be exalted. A mandate has been issued to host banquets for the lowly. A mystery has been disclosed, revealing that the kingdom of God will be built upon the lowest substrata of society.

Like Palestine, the landscape of God's kingdom is sloped so that its river flows to the lowest valleys.

The valleys are people whose lives are eroding away.

The river is mercy.

It flows freely to heal a man with dropsy . . . to host a banquet for the poor . . . to herald a kingdom for those whose only citizenship is the street.

And were it not for that river, the world would be a wasteland.

PRAYER

ear Lord,

You who had nowhere to lay your head, have mercy on those who have nowhere to lay theirs. Have mercy on those whose only home is the shelter of a cardboard box and whose only possessions are stuffed into a shopping cart.

You who experienced the hunger of the wilderness, be with them in their hunger and in the wilderness they are experiencing. Have mercy on those whose only sustenance comes from the kettle of a soup kitchen or from the kindness of a few strangers on the street.

You who were a man of sorrows, comfort them in theirs. Have mercy on those who look back on their lives with regret and remorse and grief.

As I read your Word, help me to see the landscape of your kingdom in the background. Help me to see that it is sloped toward those whose lives have become ever-widening valleys of hopelessness and despair.

Keep me from being removed from the depths of their suffering or from ever looking down on them, no matter how high I ascend in my social or economic or professional standing. But rather, Lord, melt my heart so I could be a river of mercy in their lives. . . .

An
INSTRUCTIVE MOMENT
ABOUT WATCHFULNESS

SCRIPTURE

e dressed, ready for service and keep your lamps burning, like men waiting for their master to return from a wedding banquet, so that when he comes and knocks they can immediately open the door for him. It will be good for those servants whose master finds them watching when he comes. I tell you the truth, he will dress himself to serve, will have them recline at the table and will come and wait on them. It will be good for those servants whose master finds them ready, even if he comes in the second or third watch of the night. But understand this: If the owner of the house had known at what hour the thief was coming, he would not have let his house be broken into. You also must be ready, because the Son of Man will come at an hour when you do not expect him."

Luke 12:35–40

MEDITATION

he celebration of a Hebrew wedding spans an entire week, sometimes two, with the wedding banquet frequently spilling over into the next morning. The master of the house has gone to such a banquet and left word that he wasn't sure exactly what hour he would return.

But his servants stay dressed in their work clothes, keeping the wicks of their lamps trimmed and the reservoirs filled with oil. They wait up for their master so that should he be hungry, they would be ready with food; should he be thirsty, they would be ready with drink; should he be tired, they would be ready to prepare his bed.

They wait up for him so they can serve him. They wait up for him so he won't have to come home to a dark and empty house. But most of all they wait up for him because they love him. He is a good master. His yoke is easy. His words are kind. And his love is evident in all his dealings with them.

It is only fitting that they should wait up and watch for him, putting his needs above their own.

The house is quiet when a sound from the streets is heard. "He's coming!" one of the servants calls out, and they all jump to their feet. But when they squint out the window, they see it's only a stray dog nosing around the neighborhood.

Later that night the hinges rattle, and one of them calls out: "He's at the door!" But they open the door to discover it's only the mischief of the wind.

Midnight passes and the oil in their lamps burns on into the wee hours of the morning. They are weary from the toil of the day and wearier still from staying up that night. They know their master *will* return, they just don't know when.

But the very thought of his return invigorates them, giving them a second wind for their work. They busy themselves by doing things that would please him. Little things, quietly done. Things that he alone would notice.

They build a fire in the hearth to chase away the pre-dawn chill. They want the house to be as warm and inviting as they can make it.

Finally, one of the servants hears footsteps. He alerts the others, and they gather at the door.

The door opens. The master has returned. He stands in the doorway, visibly moved by the warmth of their welcome.

It moves him so much he goes into the kitchen and takes off his festive robe, hanging it on a peg. From another peg he takes one of the servant's garments and puts it on. He tucks the flowing hem into his sash so it won't encumber him.

Then he invites the servants to recline at his table. For an awkward moment they don't quite know how to handle the honor. But he insists, and finally they settle around the low table, where he waits on them.

At first the reversal of roles puzzles them. The master of the house doing the work of an ordinary household servant? And at first they are reticent to have him wait on them. But as he goes about filling their goblets and dishing out their food, an almost giddy feeling comes over them. The master of the house, waiting on *them*!

The last time the disciples sat at a table with their master was in an upper room, where he surprised them all by wrapping a towel around his waist and washing the dirt off their feet. When he returns, he will once again dress himself to serve, waiting on those who have waited up for him.

What a surprise. What an honor. What a Savior.

When he came to this earth, he came not to be served but to serve. When he comes again, he will come as he left . . . as a master who serves.

PRAYER

ear Master who serves,

Help me to realize that you *will* return one day, just as you promised. And help me to understand that if that day doesn't dawn in my lifetime, then in death I will return to you.

Help me to realize that your arrival or my departure is always imminent. That it will come suddenly, unexpectedly, like a thief in the night. And with my realizing that, Lord, help me to live my life in a continual state of watchfulness.

Help me to be watchful for your return without being fanatical about when and how it will happen. Keep me from being fearful of whatever night may darken the world or falsely alarming others every time I hear a sound in the street or a noise at the door.

Give me such a discriminating ear that I may know the difference between your footsteps and a dog nosing around the neighborhood, between your knock and simply the wind of world events rattling the hinges.

But when you do knock, Lord, may I be among the first to greet you at the door. Dressed for work. Lamp in hand. Ready to serve.

Until then, help me to do the work that would please you—the quiet, unpretentious work of a common household servant. And grant me the grace to take delight in little things quietly done, things that your eye alone might catch and appreciate. . . .

AN
INSTRUCTIVE MOMENT
ABOUT FAITHFULNESS

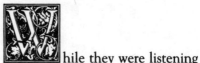

SCRIPTURE

hile they were listening to this, he went on to tell them a parable, because he was near Jerusalem and the people thought that the kingdom of God was going to appear at once. He said:

"A man of noble birth went to a distant country to have himself appointed king and then to return. So he called ten of his servants and gave them ten minas. 'Put this money to work,' he said, 'until I come back.'

"But his subjects hated him and sent a delegation after him to say, 'We don't want this man to be our king.'

"He was made king, however, and returned home. Then he sent for the servants to whom he had given the money, in order to find out what they had gained with it.

"The first one came and said, 'Sir, your mina has earned ten more.'

"'Well done, my good servant!' his master replied. 'Because you have been trustworthy in a very small matter, take charge of ten cities.'

"The second came and said, 'Sir, your mina has earned five more.'

"His master answered, 'You take charge of five cities.'

"Then another servant came and said, 'Sir, here is your mina; I have kept it laid away in a piece of cloth. I was afraid of you, because you are a hard man. You take out what you did not put in and reap what you did not sow.'

"His master replied, 'I will judge you by your own

words, you wicked servant! You knew, did you, that I am a hard man, taking out what I did not put in, and reaping what I did not sow? Why then didn't you put my money on deposit, so that when I came back, I could have collected it with interest?'

"Then he said to those standing by, 'Take his mina away from him and give it to the one who has ten minas.'

"'Sir,' they said, 'he already has ten!'

"He replied, 'I tell you that to everyone who has, more will be given, but as for the one who has nothing, even what he has will be taken away. But those enemies of mine who did not want me to be king over them— bring them here and kill them in front of me.'"

Luke 19:11–27

MEDITATION

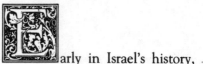arly in Israel's history,
revelation about the kingdom of God came in trickles.

> "Now then, tell my servant David,
> 'This is what the Lord Almighty says . . .
> "Your house and your kingdom will endure
> forever before me; your throne will be
> established forever." ' "

The trickles later swelled into streams that promised a
reign of unprecedented peace.

> They will beat their swords into plowshares
>   and their spears into pruning hooks.
> Nation will not take up sword against nation,
>   nor will they train for war anymore. . . .

> The wolf will live with the lamb,
>   the leopard will lie down with the goat,
>   the calf and the lion
>   and the yearling together;
>   and a little child will lead them. . . .

> They will neither harm nor destroy on all
>   my holy mountain, for the earth
> will be full of the knowledge of the Lord
>   as the waters cover the sea.

These tributaries converged at a watershed moment
when the heir to that throne was finally announced.

> "Do not be afraid, Mary, you have
> found favor with God. You will be with
> child and give birth to a son, and you are
> to give him the name Jesus. He will be

great and will be called the Son of the Most High. The Lord God will give him the throne of his father David, and he will reign over the house of Jacob forever; his kingdom will never end."

Rumors of the king rippled throughout Israel. With each sermon Jesus preached, with each miracle he performed, the tide of popularity rose. But just below the surface an undercurrent of opposition always accompanied it.

Today, as Jesus journeys toward Jerusalem, his popularity crests in the nearby city of Jericho. As he approaches that wealthy center of commerce, a blind beggar desperately calls out to him from the roadside.

"What do you want me to do for you?" Jesus asks the man whose lifeless eyes lie sunken in their sockets.

"Lord, I want to see."

"Receive your sight," Jesus tells him, "your faith has healed you." And immediately the dead eyes are brought to life.

People surge ahead with news of the healing, and the streets are aflood with anticipation. In one of the trees lining those streets is a short-statured man named Zacchaeus, the chief tax collector of the city. He too is wanting to see this miracle man, this man who would be king.

When Jesus stops at the base of the tree, asking to stay at Zacchaeus's house, a dead heart is brought to life. And the people witness yet another miracle. "Look, Lord!" Zacchaeus exclaims. "Here and now I give half of my possessions to the poor, and if I have cheated anybody out of anything, I will pay back four times the amount."

Immediately the blind man receives sight. *Here and now* Zacchaeus receives salvation. In an instant both lives are changed. It is only natural for the onlookers to assume that when Jesus goes to Jerusalem, the promised kingdom, of which these miracles are a foretaste, will appear just as suddenly.

But like the hostile subjects in the parable, the religious leaders didn't want this man to be their king. And their decision determined the course of history, sending the tortuous paths of pain to continue on their downward slope through generations to come.

Instead of peace on earth, people will continue to forge their plowshares into swords. Instead of harmony in the world, the wolf will continue to prey upon the lamb. Instead of righteousness filling the land, the knowledge of God will continue to be scarce.

And so the cries of humanity will continue to be heard. In dying moans from battlefields. In hopeless sobs from hospital beds. In tormented shrieks from insane asylums. In lonely sighs from alleyways. In tortured cries from concentration camps. In desperate pleas from famine-swept lands.

And, within a week, cries will be heard from the holy city too. For when Jesus takes that uphill road to

Jerusalem, his triumphal entry will not lead to a coronation but to a cross.

Into his face will be smashed fists of hate. Into his hand will be shoved a scepter of scorn. Onto his head will be thrust a crown of thorns.

Then this man of noble birth will depart from the earth, leaving his servants behind to carry on his work. To trade the minas of God's forgiveness for the smallest mite of faith. To invest the love of God into the world's pain.

The servants are not required to be eloquent or educated or especially gifted. Only one thing is required of them. To be trustworthy. To be people who can be depended on to work hard even in their master's absence.

In a world full of heartache and tears, it's difficult not to ask: Where is God amidst all this hurt?

God became flesh so he could come to this world of heartache and tears. He came amidst the hurt, healing blind eyes as well as broken hearts.

But the world sent him away.

The parable explains where he is now and why he is there. Which changes the question to: Where are his servants?

Where are those to whom the Savior, in his absence, has entrusted his work? To live as he lived. To love as he loved. Where are those he has called to be his hands and his voice and his feet? Extending themselves to beggars on the roadside. Calling to tax collectors in the trees. Traveling the uphill road to the cross.

As for the servants who faithfully toil amidst so much physical and emotional and spiritual pain, it is hard for them not to brood over the questions that suffering raises. But the servant has only one question to ask, really.

The question is not: Is this would-be king living in a distant country worthy of my trust?

But rather: Am I worthy of his?

PRAYER

ear Lord Jesus,

Thank you for the work you have entrusted me to do. I ask only to be worthy of that trust.

Help me to be faithful in very small things, realizing it is there where I will learn to be worthy of your trust in greater things.

Help me to be faithful to the great treasure of the gospel you have placed in my care. Keep reminding me what a wonderful message it is so I would be eager to encourage others to trade their sin for its forgiveness; their anxiety for its peace; their despair for its hope.

Help me to realize how much work there is to be done, Lord, so that when I arise, it would be to serve you, and when I lie down, it would be to rest from work well done.

For all the times I have left that work undone, Lord, I ask for your forgiveness. Forgive me for the times I have served you half-heartedly and for the opportunities to serve you that I have hidden in a piece of cloth because of my fears.

Please, Lord,

> Be with me when I am fearful
> to make me faithful.
> Be with me when I am faithful
> to make me fruitful.
> Be with me when I am fruitful
> to make me humble.

For it is only by your grace
    that I was chosen to serve you;
    only by your strength
    that I am even able to serve;
    only by *your* faithfulness
    that I am still serving you today. . . .

An
INSTRUCTIVE MOMENT
ABOUT THE PATIENCE OF GOD

e went on to tell the people this parable:

"A man planted a vineyard, rented it to some farmers and went away for a long time. At harvest time he sent a servant to the tenants so they would give him some of the fruit of the vineyard. But the tenants beat him and sent him away empty-handed. He sent another servant, but that one also they beat and treated shamefully and sent away empty-handed. He sent still a third, and they wounded him and threw him out.

"Then the owner of the vineyard said, 'What shall I do? I will send my son, whom I love; perhaps they will respect him.'

"But when the tenants saw him, they talked the matter over. 'This is the heir,' they said. 'Let's kill him, and the inheritance will be ours.' So they threw him out of the vineyard and killed him.

"What then will the owner of the vineyard do to them? He will come and kill those tenants and give the vineyard to others."

When the people heard this, they said, "May this never be!"

Jesus looked directly at them and asked, "Then what is the meaning of that which is written:

> "'The stone the builders rejected
> has become the capstone'?

"Everyone who falls on that stone will be broken to pieces, but he on whom it falls will be crushed."

The teachers of the law and the chief priests looked for a way to arrest him immediately, because they knew he had spoken this parable against them. But they were afraid of the people.

Luke 20:9–19

MEDITATION

he week before Pass-
over Jesus entered the temple courtyard and saw a
shantytown of booths and tables where the moneychangers had set up shop. The influx of pilgrims meant income
for the holy city. Opportunities to make money were
everywhere. Even in religion. *Especially* in religion.

As at the onset of Jesus' ministry, once again the
moneychangers had turned the house of prayer into a
house of profit. And once again, Jesus wouldn't stand for
it. In an outburst of rage, he kicked over their tables and
pushed down their makeshift booths.

Word of the incident echoed throughout the pillars of
the religious establishment. The commotion in the
courtyard eventually died down, but behind closed doors
the debate flared up. When all the heat had been vented,
the backroom consensus was: "This Jesus has got to be
stopped."

But stopping him would be no easy job. Any other
time it might have been, but this was Passover, and the
city was full of outsiders. How many among them were his
supporters? They didn't know, but they didn't want any
spark of theirs igniting a tinderbox of opposition.

The next day Jesus is back at that same courtyard,
teaching an informal gathering of followers, when a
ruffled bunch of religious leaders comes pecking him with
questions.

"Tell us by what authority you are doing these things.
Who gave you this authority?"

But Jesus refuses them an answer. Instead, he turns to

the people and tells them a story, demonstrating that these religious leaders are simply the last in a long line of rebels who have been challenging God's authority for centuries.

The picture Jesus paints is of Israel being God's vineyard. The religious leaders are the darkly shaded tenant farmers entrusted with the responsibility of caring for it. The image is a familiar one, coming from the prophet Isaiah:

My loved one had a vineyard on a fertile hillside.
He dug it up and cleared it of stones
    and planted it with the choicest vines.
He built a watchtower in it
    and cut out a winepress as well.

The owner of that vineyard built a hedge to keep out the foxes and wild boars that might ravage the young plants. He built a tower to watch for any thieves who might try to sneak in and steal the ripe fruit. He even built a winepress so that the fruit might be preserved.

God had done everything he could to ensure that Israel would become fruitful. With Abraham's seed God had miraculously planted the nation. As its seedling population grew, God hedged it with promises of blessing and protection. Then, after years of pruning in Egypt, God transplanted the nation to the fertile soil of Canaan in hopes of it producing a spiritual harvest so bountiful it would feed the world.

But instead Israel became a cornucopia of neglect, looking like the vineyard of the sluggard described in

117

Proverbs: "Thorns had come up everywhere, the ground was covered with weeds, and the stone wall was in ruins."

God had sent prophets to Israel to point out the holes in their spiritual walls and the places where weeds had overgrown their hearts. But the prophets were not well received.

Elijah was relentlessly pursued by Ahab and Jezebel. Zechariah was stoned to death in the temple under the reign of Joash. Jeremiah was imprisoned and later stoned. Isaiah was mocked and later sawn in two by order of Manasseh. Amos was beaten to death with a club.

Generation after generation God kept sending his servants to the vineyard. But generation after generation those servants were beaten, treated shamelessly, wounded, and thrown out.

How long should God put up with tenants who treated his servants like that? How long should he tolerate their rejection, their brutality, their sloth, their thievery, their self-indulgence?

God had been protecting the vineyard, cupping his hands around its broken walls and its crumbling watchtower. While he did this, the foxes in the Roman government and the wild boars in the military were kept at bay. But the time had come to take his hands away— just as he had done in the time of Isaiah:

"What more could have been done
    for my vineyard
    than I have done for it?
When I looked for good grapes,

why did it yield only bad?
Now I will tell you
   what I am going to do to my vineyard:
I will take away its hedge,
   and it will be destroyed;
I will break down its wall,
   and it will be trampled.
I will make it a wasteland,
   neither pruned nor cultivated,
   and briers and thorns will grow there.
I will command the clouds not to rain on it."

The vineyard of the Lord Almighty is the house
   of Israel, and the men of Judah are the
garden of his delight.
And he looked for justice, but saw bloodshed;
   for righteousness, but heard cries of distress.

The parable Jesus presents is one of judgment, reminiscent of the judgment prophesied by Isaiah. So horrible are the storied memories of that judgment that the crowd is aghast and cries out: "May it never be!"

But their appeal comes too late. The verdict has been declared; the sentence, decreed.

The parable teaches two things about God's patience. It is long-suffering. And it has its limits. God's judgment comes only after generations of his showing patience to the nation. He had sent Israel one prophet after another, until at last, he sent his own beloved Son to reason with them. But after that fateful Passover week in Jerusalem, his patience reached its end.

The parable is like no other Jesus has told. It is the only one that contains his own obituary. Imagine how he must have felt as he told his followers of his fate. What profound grief. What pain for the nation that had rejected him.

Yet still, in spite of all the raw feelings churning inside him, the Savior was early to that courtyard, reaching out to the few vines that were reaching out to him. Clearing away the weeds that had overrun their lives. Feeding the roots that were struggling for deeper soil. Encouraging the budding fruit on their eagerly branching faith.

All this the Savior did, knowing full well that in a few days the wicked tenants would throw him outside of the city walls and have him brutally killed.

Such is his faithfulness to his Father's vineyard . . . and to those in it who are eager to grow.

PRAYER

ear Lord,

Thank you for all that you've done to make my life fruitful and productive. Thank you for the hedges you've put up to protect me, for the towers you've erected to watch over me, and the furrows you've cultivated in my heart so I might be more receptive to your Word.

Help me to be a good tenant of the little acre of life you have entrusted to my care. May I work hard in that vineyard, Lord. Give me strong hands for the plow and a steadfast heart for the harvest.

Keep me from ever taking lightly your patience with my deeply rooted sin. Help me to see that no matter how long-suffering your patience is, it does have its limits. Keep me growing, Lord, so I may never have to learn what those limits are.

Thank you for all the parables in your Word that come to me cloaked as prophets. Help me to realize that however hard their message is to hear, they are sent for my good—to point out the holes in my character I am so blind in seeing and to pick out the weeds in my heart I am so fond of protecting. . . .

AN
INSTRUCTIVE MOMENT
ABOUT OUR LIVES

SCRIPTURE

emember Lot's wife! Whoever tries to keep his life will lose it, and whoever loses his life will preserve it."

Luke 17:32–33

MEDITATION

odom was a city notorious for its sin. It sat in the southernmost portion of the Jordan Valley, fermenting in its excesses, drunk with debauchery, and reeling with decadence. But because of its location, its resources, and its burgeoning population, the opportunities to make money there were sobering.

It was there that Lot made his home and raised his family. The people of Sodom could afford to eat meat every day, and they paid a premium price for prime cuts. With his shrewd mind for business, Lot soon parlayed his livestock business into an empire. Before long his attention turned to politics, and he became the leader of that city, sitting at its gate to preside over its civic affairs and to judge its legal disputes.

While Lot was busy with business and civic responsibilities, his wife was preoccupied with planning the weddings of their two daughters. She has already bought the material for the wedding garments and commissioned festive robes to be made for the guests. She is in the process now of figuring out the menu for the wedding banquet.

With her husband being such a prominent man, the guest list keeps getting longer. And so does the list of things she has to get done. But she has waited her whole life for this and relishes the responsibility. As a young girl, she had always dreamed of having daughters. As a young mother, she had always dreamed of one day hosting their weddings.

But then one night two mysterious visitors come and

shatter those dreams, warning them of the city's impending destruction.

"What? Leave town? Leave my home, my way of life? What about the weddings? What about all my plans?"

But those anxious thoughts she keeps to herself. In the gray margin before dawn her family slips surreptitiously out of the city. Lot's wife looks one last time at the home she is leaving behind, the home where she raised her daughters and lived her life, the home where her memories are stored like so many dishes in the cupboards.

The two angelic messengers lead the way, followed by Lot, then by his wife and two daughters. Their husbands-to-be stay behind, thinking it all so much religious nonsense. As she passes through the slumbering neighborhood, she begins to think it nonsense too.

After their breathless uphill trek to the small town of Zoar, the morning dawns. Slats of sun fall across the Jordan Valley, revealing an ominous billow of black clouds roiling toward the lowlands.

> Then the Lord rained down burning sulfur on Sodom and Gomorrah—from the Lord out of the heavens. Thus he overthrew those cities and the entire plain, including all those living in the cities— and also the vegetation in the land. *But Lot's wife looked back, and she became a pillar of salt.*

Those twelve words in the Old Testament paint the only picture we have of Lot's wife. Three in the New Testament put a caption beneath it.

"Remember Lot's wife."

Entombed in a pillar of salt, her life stands as a monument of warning: "Whoever tries to keep his life will lose it, and whoever loses his life will preserve it."

In that backward glance of longing for the life she left behind, Lot's wife passed from the realm of the living to the realm of parable. Though she is dead, the message of her life lives on.

Stories of people like Lot's wife make the theoretical practical. They put flesh and blood on bare-bones principles. They incarnate the Word so that it may dwell among us. To be seen and heard. To be touched and understood.

In the winding and sometimes precarious road we travel on our spiritual journey, other people's lives serve as signposts, showing us the way or the way to avoid.

The rich man and Lazarus. The tax collector and the Pharisee. The Pharisee and the prostitute.

Each points us either in the direction we should go or in the direction we shouldn't.

Of all the people's lives that have become parables, none is so instructive, so inspiring, as the life of the Savior.

He etched in our minds an image of tenderness when

he invited the children to come to him. He showed us a picture of compassion when he raised the widow of Nain's son. He silhouetted a profile of courage when he stood against the hypocrisy of the Pharisees. He sketched a mural of meekness when he rode into Jerusalem on the colt of a donkey. He sculpted the form of a servant when he washed the feet of his disciples. He drew a portrait of a friend when he surrendered his life for us. He showed us with graphic realism what it meant to love our enemies when, impaled on a Roman cross, he asked the Father to forgive those who had put him there.

He was a walking parable. Showing us how to love, how to live, and how to die. Giving us pictures that pointed the way.

Remember him.

Remember Lot's wife.

And remember that one day you will be remembered too. By someone struggling along life's path. By someone groping to find the way. By someone for whom your life has become a parable.

PRAYER

ear Lord Jesus,

Thank you for the things happening all around me, great and small, that are parables whereby you speak. Some of them are so loud I would be deaf not to hear them. Others are such whispers I have a hard time understanding what you're trying to say.

Thank you for the flowers of the field and for the birds of the air. For the warm memories of people dear to my heart. For the pictures of love on my refrigerator door.

May every moment I spend with you, O Savior, be in some way an instructive one.

Teach me to hear in such a way that the smallest seed from your Word may take root in my life.

Teach me to love my neighbor as the Good Samaritan loved his.

Teach me about life and about what really matters.

Teach me to be humble as was the tax collector who prayed in the temple.

Teach me to realize the depths of your forgiveness as did that prostitute when she washed your feet with her tears.

Teach me about the open arms of your Father and about how excited he gets when a prodigal son comes home.

Teach me how to pray.

Teach me about death and the wisdom I can learn

from realizing that one day I too will go the way of all flesh.

Teach me the power of mustard seeds and little lumps of grace when they're placed into people's lives.

Teach me to be a river of mercy so I might refresh those living in deeply rutted valleys of poverty and misery.

Teach me to be watchful for your return.

Teach me to be faithful in your absence.

Teach me to understand that though the Father's patience is long-suffering, it does have its limits.

Teach me the value of a well-lived life.

Help me to remember the lessons you have taught me in these parables, Lord. Help me also to remember that one day my life will be a parable too.

How will those around me remember me when I die? What pictures will come to their minds? What words will they use to summarize the meaning of my life?

Help me to so live my life that when they do remember me, Lord, it will be a good memory, one that in some way can help them over the rough spots in the road ahead . . . and lead them a little closer to you. . . .

"I will show you what he is like who comes to me and hears my words and puts them into practice. He is like a man building a house, who dug down deep and laid the foundation on rock. When a flood came, the torrent struck that house but could not shake it, because it was well built."